𝒯𝒲

River Uche

Women's Obsession with Shoes:
Real Stories Straight from the Sole

written and compiled by River Maria Urke

Twowolvz Creations

Women's Obsession with Shoes:

Real Stories Straight from the Sole

Copyright © 2012 by River Maria Urke

All rights reserved. No part of this publication may be reproduced, stored in a retrieval system, or transmitted by any means without prior permission in writing from the author.
Printed in the United States of America
ISBN: 978-0615640433

Twowolvz Creations
Stillwater, MN

Learn more information at:
www.riverurke.com

I Love Shoes!

❧I love buying shoes.

Dedicated to my daughter

Willow

Thank You
To my family and friends who have put up with me
for the many years I have worked on the project.

Special Acknowledgments
Thank You

To all the women I interviewed over the years to hear their shoe stories. Rose StJohn, Mary Tennis, Jessica Kramer, Marnee Forbert, Shelby Matula, Tasha Farr, Crystal Olson, Sienna Effinger, Sara Hill, Thea Ennen, Shawn, Jamie, Mary, Cindy, Rain, Lorna Voit, Rayan Stewart, and to the women that wanted to stay completely anonymous.

Contents

INTRODUCTION 11
ABOUT THE BOOK 15
HEELS 17
    LIKE MOTHER LIKE DAUGHTER 20
    RUBIES & COBBLESTONES, OH MY! 21
    A LESSON IN MOVEMENT 22
    BELLIES AND HEELS 24
    MY LUCKY BROWNS 25
    TO DANCE IN HEELS 26

FLATS 29
    MERRILL'S SHOE BOUTIQUE 32
    CURES OF LAUGHTER 33
    STICKY STICKY EARTH 34
    A VALUED SURPRISE 35
    MOCCASIN BLUES 38

SANDALS 41
    FAITHFUL AFICIONADA 44
    STILETTO STANDOFF 45
    MY ALL IN ONE'S 47
    FLORAL OF PARIS 50
    FOOTIE PORN PRINCESS 51

BOOTS 53
    ZENA MEETS ITALY 57
    BOOT SWAP WITH A QUEEN 58
    50-CENT TREASURE 59
    THE CASE OF THE PLATS 60
    SURPRISE! SURPRISE! 61

PICTURES 66
SHOE COLLECTIONS 69
ABOUT THE AUTHOR 74

Introduction

Women's Obsession with Shoes

A woman's love for shoes has no boundaries. Million's of women from all lifestyles and ages, crossing borders around the globe, care not of the necessity of shoes as much as they care of the aesthetic quality of them. The likelihood is high you know at least one friend or family member that has a love for shoes. In fact, you may be captivated yourself.

A woman's love of a pair of shoes has been known to trump comfort for many an occasion. Some women hold the view shoes are the glue that binds an outfit together, while others base their outfit on their favorite pair of trendy shoes. The fashion of trendy and designer shoes is seen in our media traveling the globe with Stilettos on top. Carrie Bradshaw from *Sex in the City* is known for her obsession with designer shoes like Manolo Blahniks and Christian Louboutin. She estimates she has a $40,000 shoe collection in her New York City apartment. Carrie is a fictional character that portrays women's obsession with shoes to an extreme. The Consumer Reports National Research Center for the shopping magazine ShopSmart conducted a poll in 2007 on women and shoes. They found that the average American woman owns 19 pairs of shoes, while 15% of women own more than 30 pairs. "Women obviously love their shoes and are willing to go to great lengths for them," said Lisa Lee Freeman, editor-in-chief of *ShopSmart*.

Why are women obsessed with shoes? When did this fascination begin? A brief look at the history of shoes along with cultural factors and philosophy will help glide us a step further in understanding women's obsession with shoes.

Women's fascination with shoes travels and twists through cultures and time with roots beginning in Ancient Egypt. Shoes displayed wealth and status within the Egyptian society. The common Egyptian on occasion wore simple leather sandals; otherwise, they wore no shoes at all. The priests and royalty used quality materials for sandals that often had curled toes and/or laced up the leg. Royalty were involved with the desire for decorative shoes contributing to the birth of the shoemaker. That seems to be the time shoes moved from being worn only for practical purposes to the elite wearing them for the aesthetics too.

Shoes have symbolized wealth and status cross culturally through time. The Greeks were known for their magnificent shoes, sandals, and boots made of high quality materials that were ornamentally embroidered and bejeweled. In the eleventh century, the Christian crusades brought back Oriental designs and fabric to Europe that influenced the elite's fashion and the shoemaker's imagination. The elite women of the 15th century in England and France wore round-toed velvet or satin mules and slippers often elaborately decorated with pearls and embroidery. (1) The seventeenth century brought the delicate Louis heel named after Louis XIV with its simple embroidery and precious stones. (2) The heel was in fashion with the elite men and women and gave the wearer the impression of height and femininity.

As time goes by, many styles of shoes continuously travel from generation to generation emerging each time with subtle changes of form and aesthetics. For example, the sandals worn in Ancient Egypt from c. 2500-1085 BC are very similar to the flip-flops we wear today. (3) In Mesopotamia period from c.1000 BC- AD 200, the first wedge heel takes shape. (4) The pointed toe we see today in various styles traces back to the twelfth to fourteen century's Pauline. (5)

The first modern heel originates towards the end of 15th century with the male court shoe Pompe. (6, 7) Chopines were invented so prostitutes and rich women's dresses were off the ground in the mucky streets of the European city. The heel height in shoes changed through the centuries from thirteen inches high to the stumpy height of a riding boot. (8) Heels in various styles became widely used by elite men and women by the eighteenth century. These are some examples of the many styles of shoes over the centuries that have entered the whirlwind of revolving footwear to come out a little altered at another time.

The turn of the century was a marking point for the history of shoes with the launch of the American factory. A mass assembly of small designer styles from factory production emerged to the public in the early 1900's. The privilege of the elite only to afford fashion and style finally ended. Styles and colors of shoes were emerging at a low price to the average women. The fashion was to have a pair of pumps to match every outfit in the 1920's. The birth of the shoe designer and the passing of the shoemaker is another feat of the early 1900's. Designers such as Perugia, Vivier, and Poiret from France and Italy designed and made shoes only affordable to the rich in the early twentieth century. Their designs were the inspirations for the styles in fashionable shoes for average women. Other designers over the decades came and went as shoes grew in the world of fashion. Today, fashionable shoes from smaller designers like Nine West are still inspired from the leading designer styles. The leading designer's are more accessible for woman today than they were in the past. Through pinching, saving, and maybe sacrificing a woman may own a pair of Christian Louboutin shoes with the red signature sole.

~

Women's obsession with shoes is rooted within an innate understanding of beauty and driven by culture and power. A culture's idea of beauty has a footing in their obsession with shoes. The perception of beauty a culture materializes integrates within the styles of the people. The Kayan people of Thailand believe neck lengthening with brass coils is beautiful with women. During the Romantic period in Europe, plumpness among women along with dainty shoes was thought beautiful. Today in Japan, United States, and other cultures around the world beauty is perceived in comparison to Western appearance of popular culture. The rave in shoes is Stilettos.

A sexual connotation lies within the beauty of shoes that is nearly universal. Women have worn high heels since the Victorian times for sensual purposes either for their pleasure or for someone else's. The desire some women have to own the perfect pair of red heels strongly symbolizes sexuality. While the arousal that Stilettos creates in men and women is seen traveling through borders and time. Today, some women are even going to the extreme and removing a bone near their pinky toe so they can fit in pointy-toed heels to feel sexy and beautiful.

The power of shoes fuels the obsession women have had through time, across borders and lifestyles. A person's natural response to be drawn to beauty along with a love of shoes is the power behind shoes. A cultures level of prestige of fine materials and high fashion has contributed to the obsession since the days of Ancient Egypt. At the turn of the 20th century, average women finally had the opportunity to let their obsession of shoes out to explore styles of mass production. There still exists a value with quality among the quantity.

The power shoes evoke is seen in some women's manner of thinking. These women bring their shoe philosophy into their outlook on their lives and the world around them. They link shoes to men in an elaborate comparison that unites them at the sole. Others have personal goals they want to achieve associated to shoes. For instance, a woman I know desperately wants to own a pair of vintage Salvatore Ferragomo shoes in her life.

~

A pair of shoes has the power to change our mood entirely about the day, an outfit, or ourselves. Many women convey that their whole demeanor can change the moment they slip their feet into a pair of heels and walk across a room. A women's clothing size may fluctuate while her shoe size is usually forgiving. This power of shoes can also be felt cross culturally with the language of shoes. A pair of shoes can bring tears or laughter between two cultures joining them together with no words.

~

The obsession women have with shoes began with royalty in Ancient Egypt and continues on today in the 21st century with women of any age and class around the globe. We live in a time where an idea of beauty has gone global. The Western conception of beauty travels through mediums of media leavings footprints others follow. These other cultures leave their mark contributing to the ever altering and revolving styles of footwear. Are shoe styles developed from a global idea of beauty then? Why do we find an obsession with shoes among different cultures and throughout time? How deep does the obsession go? A simple look at the world of fashion with designers and revolving styles through times as well as wealth and status are the first steps in simple sandals towards understanding women's obsession with shoes. A culture's idea of beauty and philosophy along with the power of shoes brings us a step closer in satin slippers. Future analysis of women's obsession with shoes will fill in the missing pieces to upgrade our footwear to the level Carrie Bradshaw from *Sex in the City* would insist upon- Stilettos.

About the Book

Women's Obsession with Shoes is a collection of twenty-one stories encompassing women, their lives, and shoes. They are stories I collected over a time span of three years. I interviewed twenty women between the ages of 17 to 67 with different lifestyles. Then, I transcribed their stories verbatim to written word with minimal editing in a concise manner for all to read and enjoy. Every story is written with the woman's voice as if she were sitting next to you telling her story.

There are four sections to the book- Heels, Flats, Boots, and Sandals. In each section, there are five stories by the women related to that particular style of shoe. The heel section has a bonus story. The stories are humorous, sexy, unusual, or a combination of the three. In addition, there are quotes scattered throughout the book from the women connecting shoes to their lives and the world around them. Some of the stories will spark memories for people and others will be entertaining in their own way.

☺ Enjoy

"Give a girl the correct footwear and she can conquer the world"

-Bette Midler

Heels

I take pride in wearing heels!

I am more confident walking down the street!

Like Mother Like Daughter

I have wanted a pair of Manolo Blahniks since I was a girl. My mother would let me wear her heels when I played dress up except for this one pair. She was adamant I couldn't even touch them without her with me. I wanted to so bad, but I knew better. When I got older I asked my mother about them. She told me those were her very special Manolo Blahniks. Once again, I made a promise to myself I would have my own pair some day. Well, like ten years ago, I was in college and did something bad so I could do just that. I took out extra loans for a trip to New York. I went during spring break to visit my cousin. My main mission was to buy my own pair of Manolo Blahniks. Of course, I went to have fun too. I was so excited we went shopping the first day for my new shoes in Manhattan at Barneys New York. I had to get a pair that was elegant and unique but not too flashy. I decided black was the best color choice and they had to be stilettos. Oh did we find me a pair of beauties. Black patent leather peep toe stilettos. The peep toe design was like no other I'd seen before. My new Manolo Blahniks were unique and elegant. I could totally wear them with a pair too. I wore those shoes my whole trip. I'm amazed I took them off to sleep. Well, its ten years later now and I still have my Manolo Blahniks. I don't get to wear them very often with my life these days. They don't work running around after my five year old and wearing them to work is out of the question. So, they are taken off the shelf and slipped on my feet when there is a special occasion. They still feel the same way or I feel the same as I did back in New York wearing them. Now, I have a daughter that plays dress up. I let her wear my heels just like my mother let me except my precious Manolo Blahniks.

Rubies & Cobblestones, Oh my!

I will never forget my Rubies I bought for when my sister and I met to share high tea at the Imperious Hotel in Victoria. I bought them off the Nordstrom rack in Minneapolis on my way to go out there. I was not thinking about the cost of the shoes or if I would wear them again. It was one of those impulsive things. Often, it is difficult for me to find a good pair of shoes in size 11 let alone a fancy pair of heels like that- bright red and embroidered with rhinestones and ridiculous flowers. They jumped of the shelf, wear me! Total attention getters and ridiculously tall heels for a six-foot woman. Lol, just a little excessive. I wore those shoes all day long, up and down the street, strutting like a peacock. I remember thinking it was the greatest. I have never worn those shoes since; actually, it was the most painful experience of my life. At the time, the emotion of loving the shoes some how masked the pain that I was feeling walking in them up and down the cobblestone streets. In a city that was all that there was, no way I was going to take off those fancy new shoes that I spent way to much money on.

A Lesson in Movement

I remember the first time I wore a pair of heels; actually, it's the first time I bought a pair of real heels too. I was living in Eugene, OR some years after High School. I had platforms before but I consider those cheater heels. Anyway, I was at this thrift store when I was dirt poor and I saw this pair of dark pink maroon vintage hush puppies. I know what you are thinking, "hush puppies don't sound that sexy," but they were hot! When I was trying them on I kept saying, "These are real comfortable" cause I wanted them really bad. I needed to keep reassuring myself that it was sensible to buy them even though they were like two dollars. Lol! I was afraid to wear them for a long time. Then, one night I went out and it was like the best feeling in the world to wear those shoes. I found out walking could be problematic but once I got dancing it was easier to dance. The way your body moves when you're in high heels. The quick little steps and the way your hips move and respond. Yeah! They are really conducive to dancing. That is when I learned about heels.

I'M ALL FOR 4 INCH

Stilettos

If you can work it!

Bellies and Heels

I have to buy a new pair of shoes every spring for my first wardrobe purchase. It sets the tone for my spring and summer wardrobes because I buy all my clothes to match my shoes. The pair I got this spring are tan peek-a-boo toed sling backs with white trim. They are like a throw back of the 40's war era shoes. I like them a lot. That reminds me of the other reason I seem to have to buy shoes every year. I have to get new shoes every time I get pregnant. Its so aggravating, my feet grow. I miss so many pairs of shoes like my silver sling backs. I searched for years and years to find an outfit to go with them but never did before I got pregnant and my feet grew out of them.

I still fit my favorite pair of shoes. They must have been a little bit big before I was pregnant the last time. They are gorgeous open toe wedge heels with leopard print and silver buckles. I love them! Even my OB doctor commented on them one day. I was nine months pregnant and still wearing those heels with my toes painted and everything.

My Lucky Browns

I guess to start I have to explain that I was in an extra curricular activity called Decca and we had taken 2nd place in a state competition for running a mock coffee shop for a year. Winning second advanced us to the international level and we were going to Atlantic, Georgia to compete against the world. When we got down to Atlanta, we ended up walking almost everywhere. Thank goodness, the pumps I got for the trip were super comfortable. That night Billy, a Decca alumnus, took my shoes and said he was going to put luck all over them. He never told me what he did but, I do know the next day in the finals, we did our presentation perfect. I kept thinking as we walked away that it was the lucky pumps. The next day we made the top ten. I'm like, "You guys these are my lucky shoes, these are my lucky heels! We are going to win!" We got up on stage and they called third place and then second place. We were freaking out there was only first place left. They called first place in the world and we won. I know now we earned that reward but those shoes will forever be my lucky browns.

Bonus~ my shoe story

To Dance in Heels

I joke I found my feminine side at the age of thirty. I began learning how to put on make-up, and get all dolled up for an evening. In no time at all, I came to realize I loved shoes, especially the feeling of dancing in heels. Some people might have thought I drank some funky drink or motherhood had put a spell on me transforming the woman they knew suddenly overnight. A woman they last remembered as a shoeless, nonchalant dresser strolling up to them outside the coffee house wearing Nine West pumps, a pretty dress, and a splash of lipstick. I believe it was simply my time to bloom.

I had three years of enjoying the feeling of walking down the street wearing heels before my life dramatically changed physically. I reached a point with my disease and I became disabled from the progression of Multiple Sclerosis. My balance and leg strength had worsened and I had to start walking with a cane. Wearing heels occasionally turned into a pleasure of my past and a goal to be reached with patience and hard work. Once, I told my physical therapist that wearing heels is one of my personal goals. She looked at me shaking her head not agreeing with my choice at all. I keep that goal to myself now and I tell her my other goal of dancing.

Over the years, my style of dress continues to integrate a feminine twist to its funky fusion of Trendy and Bohemian style. My love for shoes has continued growing with knowledge and new pairs even with my shoe limitations. I focus my captivation on low heels, non-risk boots, and cute flats depending on how I am physically any given day. I do test my limits with height from time to time as I strive to reach my goal to dance in heels again.

*You never truly know someone

until you've walked a mile in her shoes.*
-author unknown

My relationship with shoes has been a lot like my motto for life,

"It's an exercise in endurance."

Wouldn't you know it turns out there are comfortable shoes out there.

Flats

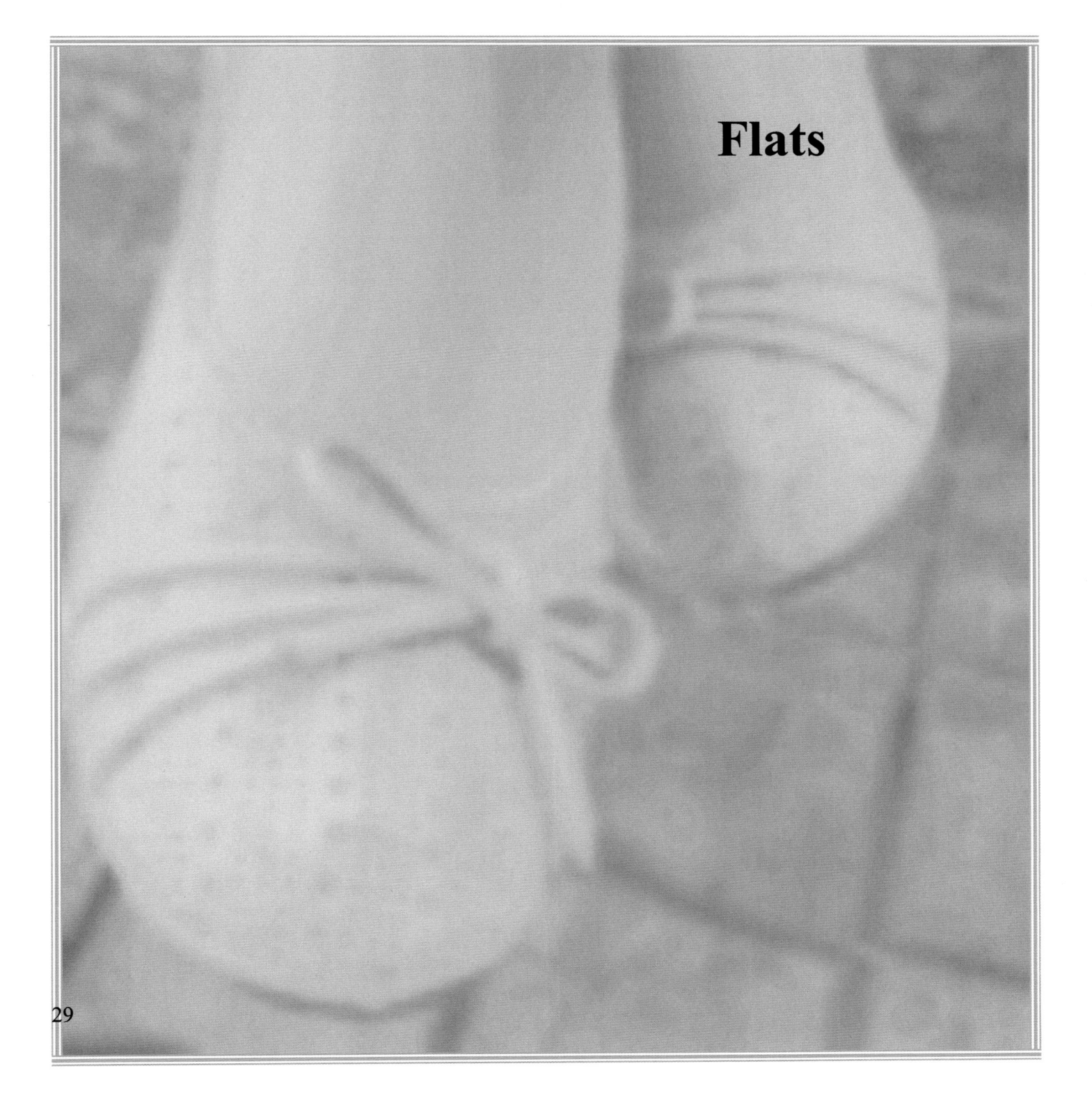

You can learn a lot about a person

by what shoes they are wearing.

Merrill's Shoe Boutique

There was a woman named Merrill that had her own shoe boutique. She was known to find the unique. I was probably 23 at the time and I had a disposable income. I was working my first career position and I had no debts yet. Most of the time I went to admire her shoes. Then one day, I went into Merrill's and there was this pair of shoes that were candy apple red like nothing I have ever seen before. I had to have them. They were like Espadrilles but more like a flat, hot red with silver heels and silver straps that you would wrap around your angle and tie in the back. I found a way to not only wear them in the evening but I was able to incorporate them into my wardrobe for daytime too. That summer I was working for a bank. As outrageous as it might sound now, I would wear my red-hot shoes with the silver straps to the bank with my black walking shorts, a white shirt and a red leather belt. Lol! I cannot believe I got away with wearing them at work.

Cures of Laughter

I have a great shoe story from when I went to Japan on a glass scholarship from the Glass Art Society to study glass making throughout the country. I was in Tokyo; no it was Osaka, visiting a friend who taught English to adult women. He brought my girlfriend and I to their classroom and introduced us to all these wonderful middle-aged very traditional Japanese women. We were invited to one of their homes. They dressed us in a full Kimono, tied the Obi for us, and we studied the tea ceremony. The women walked us through the tea ceremony in the tearoom and taught us the proper way to turn the bowl and mix the tea. They taught us rituals associated with the traditional tea ceremony. The women were just shocked by my size, "such a big American woman, so tall. Nobody is this tall here." They just loved it. Everyone seemed really shocked by it. I would walk the subways and there'd be gangs of Japanese boys coming at me. If I saw that here I would be scared but there I felt no threat at all. They all looked at me like I was this Amazon and I guess I was one there. Lol! Anyway, back to the shoes, after dressing us in the full Kimono and Obi the women brought out the little shoes for us to put on. It was the funniest thing ever; my hand was the same size as the shoe. Lol! So, as a joke I wore the shoes on my hands. I couldn't even fit two toes into the very front of these little flat bamboo wooden shoes with a little perpendicular heel in the back and a little leather strap on the front. It was hilarious. Lol! The picture is worth a thousand words and I have the picture. They photographed me standing their laughing trying to put my feet into these shoes, trying to wedge my toes into them and 75% of my foot is hanging off the back of it. They thought that was just the funniest thing they had ever seen. This big American woman trying to squeeze her giant feet into these tiny little quant shoes. It made a great laugh for everybody there. Otherwise, we didn't know each other or each other's cultures or have anything in common but a good laugh about a good pair of shoes among women is cross-cultural.

Sticky Sticky Earth

This is my mother's shoe story from when she was a teenager in the 70's. I heard her tell it so many times. So, one day she steels her sister's Earth shoes to go and impress a guy. Her best friend and her take a bus to go meet this guy and his friend. They sit right in front of the heater on the bus to stay warm cause it was winter time. They get off the bus at their stop, my mom's feet instantly freeze to the sidewalk, and she falls out of her shoes onto the ground. By chance, that guy is walking up to them at the same time. My mom was laughing so hard, she has the loudest laugh ever too, and her friend was trying to rip the shoes off the sidewalk. This guy walks bye and kind of looks down at her and just keeps going. He has a look of, "what is wrong with these two?" My moms like rolling around on the sidewalk and both of them are laughing hysterically. She walked right out of her shoes onto the sidewalk. Lol! Her plan to impress the guy didn't work out. I don't think he ever talked to her again.

A Valued Surprise

I have a pair of shoes upstairs in a box that doesn't ever see the light of day any more. They are a pair of gunmetal colored Doc Martin Mary Janes. You see, the whole time I was in High School I wanted Doc Martins because they were like the thing to have but they were to expensive. My mom would never fork over that kind of money for shoes and I didn't have the will power to save up for them. So, I had been at a Fish concert and we were on our way back to New Hampshire. We stopped at this awesome shoe store somewhere in Massachusetts. I think my boyfriend knew about it or something. Anyways, they had a pair of Doc Martins in a window. They were slightly discolored but it made them look cooler. They ended up being on sale for like 45 dollars, my size and everything. I think that was probably all the money I had at the time but I thought, "I have to get these shoes." So I did. I put them on and didn't take them off; seriously, I wore them every day for probably like three years. I wore them in all kinds of weather in New Hampshire and then I took them to Italy with me. When I was in Italy, I noticed the first thing people look at when they meet you is your shoes. Not surprisingly, it's the same when an Italian man is sizing you up too. They can know exactly where you are from by your shoes. They'd look at my shoes, look up and say hello in English if I didn't answer they'd try hello in German. Anyway, those shoes got me through Italy, then I wore them out west, and brought them with me to MN. I got my first kitchen job making pizzas and those things just got trashed. I was wearing them all the time in snow and everything. They ended up getting caked with flour and just totally wrecked. I wore those suckers until I couldn't wear them anymore. I had them repaired twice. They are just filthy, moldering and I still have them in a box because they have so much value to me. They went through so much with me, you know. I can't believe I've kept them its like this nasty surprise, you open the box and your like what the hell. Honestly, they look like they are 100 years old.

Everyday when I wake up and pick out what shoes I'm going to wear

it's like I'm looking at a scrapbook:

*Each pair of shoes
has an experience, a memory,
a time, a place, or
a person associated with it.*

Moccasin Blues

I dance at Pow Wows every summer. I am a Fancy Shawl dancer. Every year, we look for a new pair of homemade beaded moccasins for me that fit well and have a good design on them that match my outfit. We always look for them at Grand Portage Pow Wow because they have really good high quality moccasins up there. One year, we finally found the perfect pair. They were a tan leather with a white tongue and beaded flowers in pink, green, and purple. So, I get my new eighty-dollar moccasins and I was so excited. They were spendy but it was worth it. They were comfortable and had really nice beadwork on them. When we got back to the camp I had to wear them for a little bit. After awhile a bunch of my friends came by the camp and I decided to go walk around the campgrounds with them. I didn't want to ruin my moccasins walking down trails and stuff so I took them off. I set them by my chair next to the campfire. So, I walk around and come back how ever many hours later. First thing, I go to my chair and my new moccasins aren't there. So I'm searching around the fire looking for my moccasins in the dark and I can't find them. I was freaking out because there are at least a couple thousand people at this Pow Wow. It's kind of an open campground where people walk through who evers camp spots and they could have been taken. I was freaking out looking all over the place. I looked through my tent, my suitcase where my outfit was packed, and I looked through the car. I couldn't ask any of the adults if they'd seen them cause they were all sleeping. So, I just kind of put it off for the night. I figured I'd have to look for them in the morning when it was light out. The next morning, I get up and I'm walking around asking everyone if they'd seen my moccasins and every buddy's telling me no. I was really mad because they were really nice and they were expensive. I finally go up to my mom and ask her if she'd seen my moccasins. She gives me this attitude like you lost your moccasins already we just bought them yesterday and dadadaa. She was so mad. So, here comes one o'clock, which is when we have our Grand Entry. I'm getting ready and I'm searching for my new moccasins because I don't want to wear my old holy ones I want to wear my new ones with beadwork. I go tell my mom I can't find my moccasins; I really need to find them. She goes, "They are in my tent right by my suitcase and if you ever lose them or leave them out again I will take them away for good." Everyone in the camp knew what my mom had done and still said no when I asked them if they'd seen them. So, I finally got my moccasins, I put sage and cedar in them, and I got to dance in them in Grand Entry. If I would have put them away to begin with then I would have been able to get all my stuff done. But no they were in mom's tent and she wouldn't tell me where they were because she wanted me to realize how important it was not to lose them. I know now.

*I still have my feet on the ground,
I just wear better shoes.*
>   by Oprah Winfrey

Sandals

Footwear:
    the salvation you walk on!

Faithful Aficionada

I never knew how many pairs I had until my granddaughter asked, "Grandma, why do you have so many shoes?" I knew she meant the row of Birkenstocks downstairs. I thought I had more but six pairs lined up looks like a lot. There is a black pair and a brown pair that are old and recycled from last year that I wear and then the new ones. I have two pairs that are black and one of them is a feminine or delicate style. Then I have two tan ones with two and three straps. The thing is that's about all I wear and I have been wearing them since the 70's. I don't want to deal with it and I don't like to shop. Some say it's because I'm creative in all other areas of my day. I do know after I went to this wedding four years ago and I wore heels that I decided that night it was the last time. I refuse to be uncomfortable. Now I just wear my feminine Birkenstocks with a dress and dark stockings. Nobody ever notices what I'm wearing on my feet because I don't go dancing. On a regular day, I wear my old Birkenstocks shopping and walking the dog and the brand new ones when I want to dress nicer. I save money with my system. It's actually very economical.

Birkenstocks are me.

Stiletto Standoff

I love heels. Actually, it's all I ever wear. I have been only wearing heels since I was sixteen. Not long ago, I bought these new sandals online. Killer, killer shoes. I love them to death. They are 5 ½ inch black platform stilettos with a band around the ankle. So, there was this night a couple of months ago or so, we were all down at the club dancing and I'm wearing my new shoes. It was shot night. Everyone was buying random shots and I got in a fight with the boyfriend. I got mad at him. It was really weird. We don't get mad at each other. I don't remember any of it. I guess I was pushing him against the wall. He said when he looked at me he didn't even know who I was. Yeah, it was really bad. I haven't drank for 58 days because of it. It was like OK time to get it under wrap. So, then the cops drive by and we are out on the sidewalk and I'm pushing him. They stopped and tried to tell me to do something. I wasn't having any of that. I ended up taking on two police officers in 5 ½ inch stilettos. I got tazered. They dropped me to the ground and I ate gravel. This is all in my shoes. I was kicking at them. I don't remember any of this. I have a six-page police report to prove it. They could not cuff me or control me. Two grown men. I took on two grown men, uniformed, armed men. So, they finally get me in the squad, cuffed and they're bringing me to jail. I had never been to jail. I have never had any legal problems. I had a spotless record. This is a horrible story and a great story. I'm looking back laughing at it. Well sort of, I'm getting there. At least I learned from it. Well the cops are driving me from A to B like 20 minutes and I'm calling Internal Affairs getting them fired. I was even tightening up my own handcuffs because I want them to get in trouble. OK back to the shoe part of it. I get to the jail. They wont let me wear my shoes in the holding cell. I freak out again because I am not taking my shoes off. "These are my shoes, these are my babies and you want me to take them off," I say to them. It's amazing what they can do to you. Yeah, they got my shoes off me and they put me in.

the holding cell. I'm surrounded by cement with this little window and I have my belt. I have my 8- pound pewter belt buckle with agates on and not my shoes. So, I take my belt off and I'm banging on the glass with it. "You let me keep this and not my shoes." Yeah, I'm going off about my shoes again. Lol!

My All in One's

I was going to Europe for the forth time and needed a pair of all in one sandal that were comfortable for the trip. See, when you're in a European city, you walk and walk then without going back to your hotel to change you're going out to dinner or out to lunch. You kind of want to have a versatile pair of shoes that can do multiple things. I tried on Chaco's but they weren't my style and you can't dress them up or anything. I was looking all over. Tivas looked to hiking-ish. I have to look cute every day too. So, I was looking on line and I found these Birkenstocks. I was like, "Oh yeah typical," but they were really cute. They have a leather strap that goes up the center and they were black. They looked dressy enough plus they'll be comfortable because they're Birkenstocks. I can get behind that. So, I had to go all the way down to the cities to try them on and figure out the right size. I wasn't going to buy a pair of really expensive shoes online if I didn't know how they fit. They fit and looked great so, I went back online and ordered them because it was much cheaper that way. The Birkenstocks performed wonderfully on my trip. They were the versatile pair of shoes I needed for Europe.

Often, I look at dating kind of like trying on shoes at the shoe store.

You know some of the shoes really look

and feel good at the store

but god you take them home

and then out in public

and they just look like hell

and they hurt your feet.

Often, men like an uncomfortable pair of shoes

may look real good but really don't quit fit.

Floral of Paris

First, I should tell you I have 152 pairs of shoes. I have always had a large amount of shoes. My latest big purchase was six months ago when I had an interview to be a broadcaster on a cable television network. I was really excited about it cause that's what I want to do is be on television and in film. So I went to Barneys New York, a very fancy store and I found this floral dress very unlike my solid colors. Usually, I am classical and timeless in my clothing choices but not that day. I wanted a trendy floral dress that happened to cost a couple hundred dollars. I needed some shoes to go with this dress too. That was obvious, right. So, I head to this fancy department store to look at the shoes and I find a pair that matched the dress perfectly. A pair of pink heeled sandals from Paris, a total French brand. Super, super cute. They have this woven fabric on the side, so there's not a single heel but a connected 3-inch heel, almost platform 70's thing with this pink fabric that goes over the toe. They were on sale for 150 bucks and I didn't even blink an eye. I'm like, "Yeah, that's not a problem." I will spend that much on shoes. I didn't get the job but I looked good and I have a really cool pair of shoes for my collection.

Footie Porn Princess

At one point, I was selling Vintage clothing on Ebay for a living. A lot of the time I would model the clothing that I was selling for the pictures. I remember one picture impaticular brought my selling to another level you can say. Lol! I was wearing an outfit for sale and sitting on the back of my car with a pair of white thong sandals on my summer feet. Well, I starting getting emails from guys telling me about my feet. I thought that was very strange cause its something I had never really thought about before. They started explaining to me how I guess EBay is a really big place people look for foot fetish paraphernalia. I couldn't help looking into it and starting to sell stuff on EBay for lots and lots of money. Basically, all they would ask for is the shoes and a picture(s) of you wearing them. I think the most I made off of one pair was $500. I started posting an auction listing for them where people would bid on the shoes and contact me privately. You have to be really careful cause there are rules on EBay. You would have to send the pictures afterwards cause they don't allow you to sell pictures above the knee and that type of thing. The money depended on what the the guy and sometimes the gal wanted but on average $50. The real money came from the auction stuff and if the big things they looked for like sandals, socks, or thigh high stockings were part of the package. Heels are not required. In fact, the picture that started this career off are totally flat little summer thong sandals. Where they are really particular is about the person's feet. The woman needs to have small feet with long toes and the big turn on is that the 2nd toe is longer than the 1st toe. Which is all something I have. Lol! I had to learn all of their likes and dislikes to be good at the bussiness. I noticed an Accountant stereotype of people that were usually quite and shy in their everyday life. Believe it or not, I actually met some really great people. The way you think about it compared to other fetishes its very docile. It seems they don't feel comfortable telling the people they are with about their foot fetish because society doesn't really look at it quit the same way as they look at feet.

I admit,
I have a shoe problem.
It's bad too!

Boots

*Men I may not know,
but shoes,
shoes I know.*
— Carrie Bradshaw

Shoes change everything!

You can base an entire outfit out of just the shoes on your feet.

Zena meets Italy

One of my all time, favorite pairs of shoes are these Italian green leather boots with leather straps that lace all the way up the boot. They have thick 3-inch heels with a rounded point. I call them my Zena boots. I bought them when I was part of the foreign student exchange program in Italy. They were so ridiculously expensive. I had to have them. I didn't care. They don't make boots like that here. That's an Italian thing. It was like my last week there. I walked right by this store and stopped in mid step. I was like, "Oh, those beauties are mine. That's it I'm going to blow the rest of my money on those cause I'm here and I can and I want too."

Boot Swap with a Queen

I'm a rather tall woman with large feet and finding a really kick ass pair of bitch boots can be very difficult. So, when you find them you have to go for it. I have these great lavender knee high boots. They zip up and have 2 ½ high spiked heels. Well, OK there was this time when lets say the boots had an unforgettable night. We were at Nye's Polonaise for a friend's after wedding party. The bride was there and all the drag queens too. One of the drag queens came up to me and said, "Honey, where did you get those boots?" I think she thought I was also a drag queen because I was hovering at 6 foot 2 or 6 foot 3 in heels all dressed to the nines. Nye's Polonaise is where many of the Drag Queens hang out. I could easily be mistaken to be one; especially, when you dress and act a little over the top like I tend to do after a great reception. Anyway, she wanted to try on my boots and I thought her shoes were fabulous too. So we traded shoes for the night. We danced in each other's shoes. It was great. I probably would have forgotten that entire wedding reception because for the most part it was uneventful except for the unforgettable boot swap with the drag queen.

50-cent Treasure

So, I like to treasure hunt. A different kind of treasure hunting then you might think. I find unique surprises at second hand stores and rummage sales. My mother raised me second hand shopping. It's something I've always done. But anyways, my shoe story. One day, I found a pair of authentic pink cowgirl boots for fifty cents. They fit me perfect. The only problem was the color. I'm not much of a pink person. Now I will wear pink here and there, but at that point not at all. It was my first endeavor into the world of pink. I couldn't walk away from an authentic pair of cowgirl boots especially that they were 50 cents. So, I got them and I would wear them here and there. I think it was around six months to a year before this new fashion wave blew in. Suddenly, cowgirl boots were in fad. So I'd wear them when I felt like it. I think at that time I had a cowgirl hat too. It was pretty cool. Both my daughter and I had cowgirl hats. When we traveled we always wore our hats. Anyway the boots. When I would wear them everybody and their mama would ask me where I got those boots. I would just smile happily and say, "I got them for fifty cents. They are one of my treasures."

The Case of the Plats

I had like 13 pairs of really nice platform boots at one time. I bought every type of platform shoe you could find when I first moved to Saint Louis. I'd wear them everywhere even at work making click clack sounds down the hall. Then I got pregnant. I kept wearing all my platforms until I was 3 months pregnant or so. One day, my now ex-husband and I were walking through the grocery store, my ankle kind of gave out and I almost fell. Two days later, I came home from work and all my platform boots were gone. My ex-husband took them and threw them away. All of them. Can you say controlling? I only had one pair left. The pair of boots I had worn to work that day. After I had my daughter, the one pair I did have didn't fit me anymore. I was almost a whole shoe size bigger. My feet grew so all those platforms wouldn't have fit me anyway. So, I couldn't like hate him for it. I could still be pissed because of the principal of it and that I had a lot of money invested in those shoes. Man, I was buying nice shoes. Everyone at work knew I was coming cause they'd hear clunk clunk down the hall. I thought I was so stylish.

Surprise! Surprise!

I went shopping; which is really strange cause I hate shopping, but I wanted too. I went to the discount shoe store and straight back to the sales rack. Where, you know, it seems all the really cute shoes are in like size 5 to 7 and I think I wore a size 7 when I was 12. So here I have to travel over to the 9- 91/2, I'm still trying to convince myself that I'm not quit a 10. It's like a mine field back there with shoes all over the place. Do you know about ladies in discount shoe stores? They're beasts. lol! Lately, I've been a renegade to the flat shoe because of back problems, which again not fun and harder to find cute shoes- flat. So, I'm trying to switch over and transition into good flat shoes for working in and walking in. So, that's what I am supposed to be looking for but... I find this pair of supper sexy stiletto heeled black boots with a little silver buckle on the side. I try them on and they are soo fantastic. They've got the supper doper long points that look ridiculous and I just look great in them. I'm strutting around the store in these shoes and loving it. I buy the boots knowing full well I'm going to hear an ear full from my mother the moment that I wear them with her around. I get home, you know how it is when you get something new, you want to concoct a reason to wear it, and there's nothing going on that night. I couldn't come up with any excuse to wear these boots out in public and strut around all sexy. So this fella I'm seeing that's a bit nerdy is coming over. I think to myself perfect because I can wear the black boots for him. He comes over and we are just hanging out up in my room. He's laying on the bed kind of laughing and talking with me with his hands up behind his head- chilling. Out of the blue, I tell him to close his eyes and he's got to keep them closed. I pull the shoes out of the box, I take everything off, and then I put on the boots. So, I'm buck naked except for these fantastic stiletto heeled pointed boots. I crawl up on the bed and I straddled him with my foot on his chest like I'm making a claim. He doesn't even open his eyes, he just smiles this big wide smile and he reaches up and feels for the shoe and then he opens his eyes and you can take it from there.

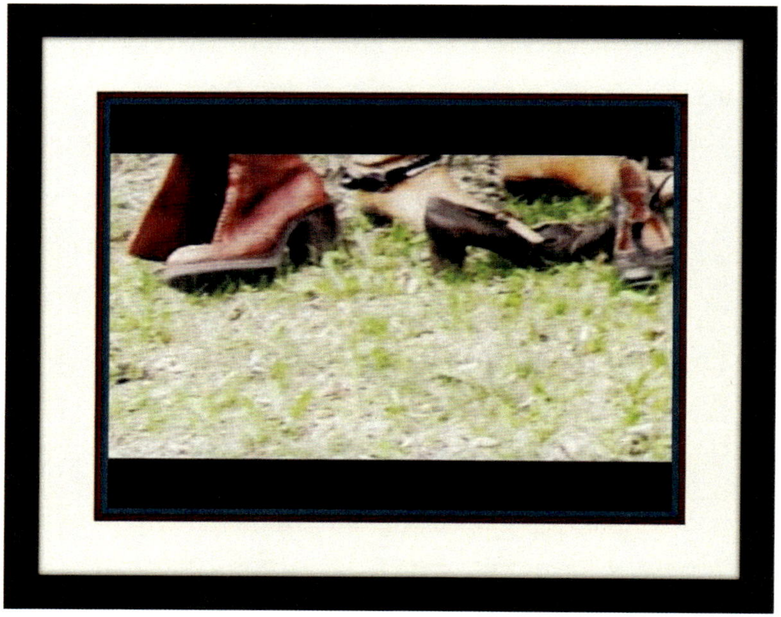

*It doesn't matter how
fat, short, thin, or
tall you are*

Shoes are always Forgiving

Respect

      Your Shoes!

Respect Yourself!

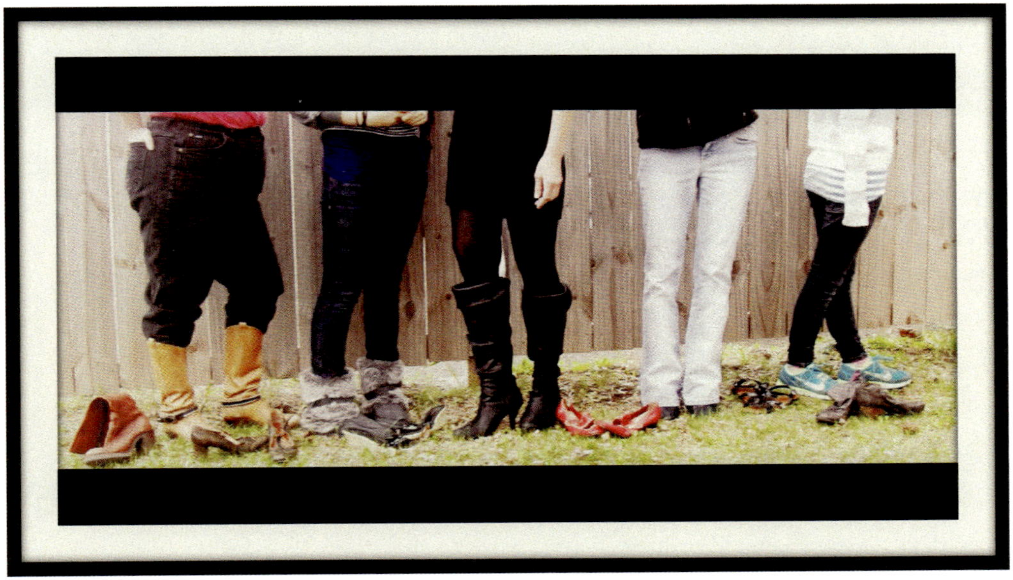

Pictures

* From the Introduction page 9;

1) 15th Century-round-toed velvet mules-
   http://en.wikipedia.org/wiki/1550%E2%80%931600_in_fashion#Footwear
2) 18th Century- Louis heel-   http://en.wikipedia.org/wiki/1750%E2%80%931775_in_fashion#Shoesh

* Comparative styles through time

3) Ancient Egypt from c. 2500-1085 BC- sandals and flip-flops
   http://www.vannacalzature.it/Storia_inglese/egizi_inglese.htm
4) Mesopotamia period from c.1000 BC- AD 200- wedge heels
   http://www.egyptsearch.com/forums/ultimatebb.cgi?ubb=get_topic;f=8;t=007057
5) 14th Century- Paulaine pointed toe
   http://oldrags.tumblr.com/post/5324037077/shoe-late-14th-century-museum-of-london-these
6) 15th Century- women's mule shoe Chopines/ heels
   http://en.wikipedia.org/wiki/1500%E2%80%931550_in_fashion#Footwear
7) 15th Century- male court shoe Pompe
   tinatarnoff.typepad.com
8) Heel height- thirteen inches high Chopines and Stilettos
   http://blog.aurorahistoryboutique.com/history-of-renaissance-shoes-an-exaggeration-of-style/

   http://en.wikipedia.org/wiki/Chopine
9) Chopines- 16th Century
   http://en.wikipedia.org/wiki/File:Chopine_(PSF).jpg

pictures pages 57 & 59 by River Urke

Shoe Collection: p 64-67

1 Rachel Zoe's Shoe Collection.

http://thegcblog.com/category/shoes/

2 Paula Abdul and her shoes

http://www.decorpad.com/photo.htm?photoId=954

3 The closet of Carrie Bradshaw.

http://jgkitchens.blogspot.com/

4 Christina Aguilera's shoe closet.

http://goddesstasha.com/onlyhighheelsblog/2009/11/19/christina-aguileras-well-organized-shoe-closet/

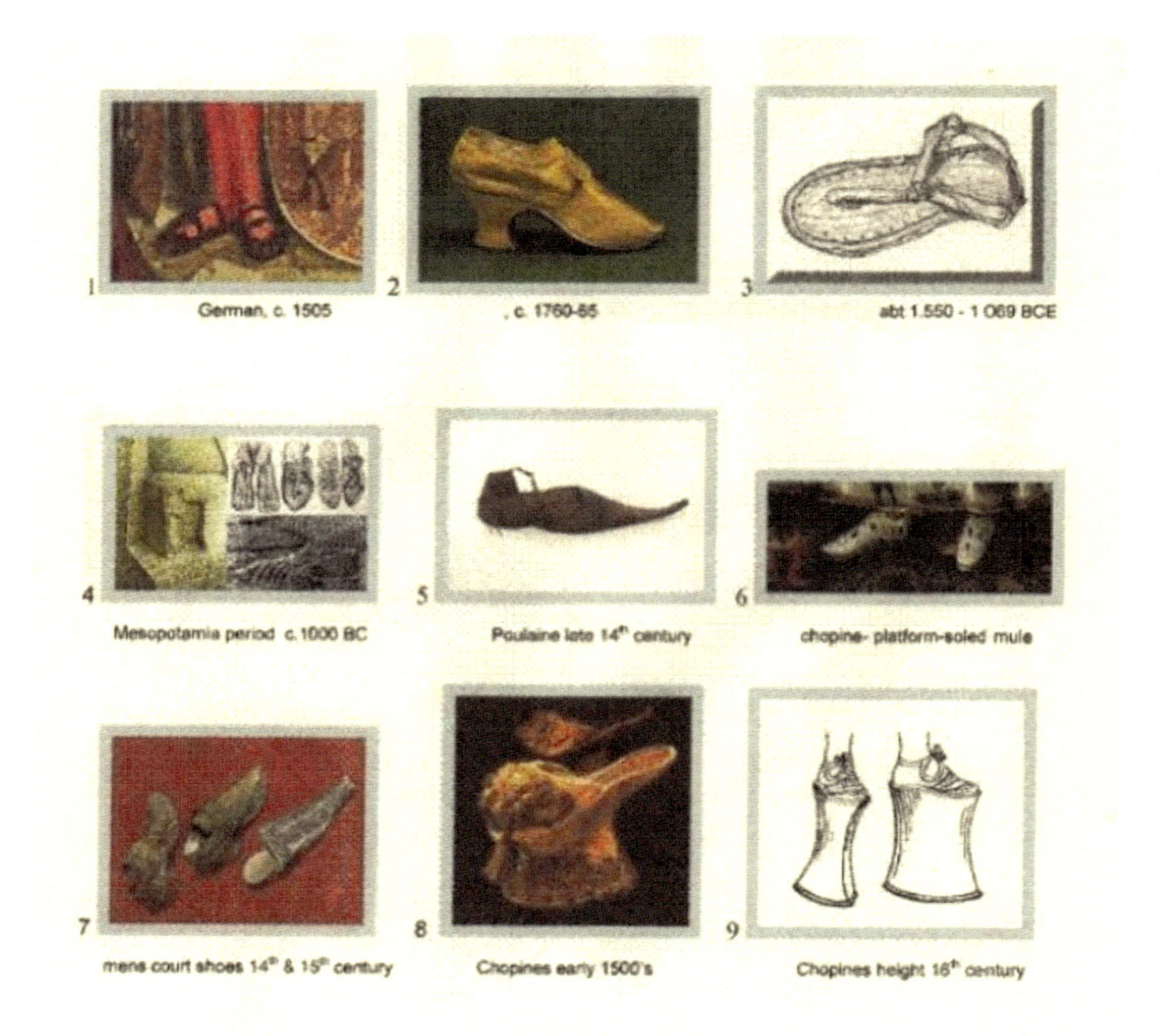

1. German, c. 1505
2. c. 1760-85
3. abt 1,550 - 1,069 BCE
4. Mesopotamia period c. 1000 BC
5. Poulaine late 14th century
6. chopine- platform-soled mule
7. mens court shoes 14th & 15th century
8. Chopines early 1500's
9. Chopines height 16th century

Shoe Collections

Rachel Zoe's Shoe Collection

Paula Abdul and her shoes

The closet of Carrie Bradshaw.

Christina Aguilera's shoe closet.

Bibliography

Carrie Bradshaw. Wikipedia.

<http://en.wikikpedia.org/wiki/Carrie_Bradshaw

Cosgrave, Bronwyn. The Complete History of Costume & Fashion: From Ancient Egypt to the Present Day. Great Britain: Octopus Publishing Group Limited, 2000.

Kayan. Wikipedia

<http://en.wikipedia.org/wiki/Kayan_%28Burma%29

Reilly, Maureen. *Hot Shoes: 100 Years.* Atglen, PA: Schiffer Publishing, Ltd, 1998

Shoe Designers. Designer History

<www.designerhisory.com/historyoffashion/shoesframe.html

Shopsmart shoe poll finds women own an average of 19 pairs of shoes. Chatham Journal Weekly <http://www.chathamjournal.com/weekly/living/consumer/women-own-many-shoes-71112.shtml (12 November 2007)

Webb, Zoë Thomas. *Shoes: The Complete Sourcebook.* London: Thames & Hudson Ltd, 2005.

About the Author

River has the heart of a poet and the eyes of an artist. She lives in the US along the St Croix Valley in the state of Minnesota with her daughter Willow, her boyfriend Tommy, and all their pets. A cat burglar named Brownie, their omega dog, Odie, and Mister Big Balls, the rat.

River is a published poet, writer, and Senior Editor of the monthly journal, *The River*. Her adventurous spirit carries her writings through genres while her necessity to create blends with many mediums. River's writings and artistic touches reflect her Ojibwe and Celtic heritages along with her life as a mother, an abstract thinker, and a thirty something woman. She believes life without laughter is no life at all.

River has the training and experience to gather stories by interviewing individuals through her degrees in Anthropology and American Indian Studies. She used those tools when gathering shoe stories from the women. Then she delivered their words onto paper in a concise manner for all to read and enjoy.

Once a friend asked River how she came up with the idea behind *Women's Obsession with Shoes*. She told her the idea came one day while she was daydreaming about dancing in heels again. When by chance two of her passions in life, writing and people's stories, came into her thoughts and the idea of WOS was born. It made total sense to bring them together to form a book.

There are links to River's works on page 76.

Double by River Urke

Writings by River- Works by River Urke.

http://riverurke.com

The River – Art & Literary Journal
http://theriverjournal.org/

A Pocket of Agates- Poetry by River
http://riverurkepoetry.wordpress.com/

Twowolvz Creations- Design & Publishing Co.
http://twowolvz.com

A girls most beautiful outfit ever is charisma
the prettiest accessory is
smile
and the best pair of heels is confidence.

-author unknown